Y0-CDK-986

# The Populist Party

## A Voice for the Farmers in an Industrial Society

Bernadette Brexel

ROSEN CLASSROOM
PRIMARYSOURCE™

Rosen Classroom Books & Materials™
New York

Published in 2004 by The Rosen Publishing Group, Inc.
29 East 21st Street, New York, NY 10010

Copyright © 2004 by The Rosen Publishing Group, Inc.

First Edition

All rights reserved. No part of this book may be reproduced in any form without permission in writing from the publisher, except by a reviewer.

**Library of Congress Cataloging-in-Publication Data**

Brexel, Bernadette.
The Populist Party: a voice for the farmers in an industrial society / by Bernadette Brexel.—1st ed.
    p. cm.—(America's industrial society in the 19th century)
Summary: Examines the history of the Populist Party in the United States, which was formed in 1892 to represent the needs of working-class citizens and bring about reform in government, big business, and labor laws.
Includes bibliographical references and index.
ISBN 0-8239-4029-2 (lib. bdg.)
ISBN 0-8239-4284-8 (pbk.)
6-pack ISBN 0-8239-4296-1
1. Populist Party (U.S.)—History—Juvenile literature. [1. Populist Party (U.S.)—History. 2. Populism. 3. United States—Politics and government—1865–1933.]
I. Title. II. Series: America's industrial society in the 19th century.
JK2372.B74 2004
324.2732'7—dc21

                                                       2002155515

*Manufactured in the United States of America*

**On the cover:** first row (from left to right): steamship docked at a landing; Tammany Hall on election night, 1859; map showing U.S. railroad routes in 1883; detail of banknote, 1822, Bank of the Commonwealth of Kentucky; People's Party (Populist) Convention at Columbus, Nebraska, 1890 (also shown enlarged); Republican ticket, 1865. Second row (from left to right): William McKinley gives a campaign speech in 1896; parade banner of the Veterans of the Haymarket Riot; Alexander Graham Bell's sketch of the telephone, c. 1876; public declaration on how government can crush monopolies; city planners' illustration of Stockton, California; railroad construction camp, Nebraska, 1889.

**Photo credits:** cover, p. 18 © Nebraska State Historical Society Photograph Collections; p. 6 © Denver Public Library, Western History Collection, H.S. Poley, P-979; p. 8 courtesy of *New York in the Nineteenth Century*, Dover Publications, Inc.; p. 11 © Corbis; pp. 12, 21, 26 © Culver Pictures, Inc.; pp. 14, 17, 25 © Library of Congress, Prints and Photographs Division; p. 22 © Bettmann/Corbis.

**Designer:** Tahara Hasan; **Editor:** Mark Beyer; **Photo Researcher:** Peter Tomlinson

# Contents

# 1
# Life in the 1800s

The 1800s were a time of great change in America. In 1800, the new American government was less than thirty years old. Americans were still settling the wild lands of the western frontier. Roads were being built between the states to allow for better business, travel, and trade. People traveled by horse or horse-drawn carriage.

New inventions made life and business easier during the mid-1800s. The steam locomotive and the railroad were two such inventions. The railroad system began operating in the middle 1800s. Companies built railroads between towns and cities. People liked trains because they could ship goods more easily than by using early roads. Many early roads were made from dirt, and as a result, bad weather could keep a shipment from its scheduled arrival.

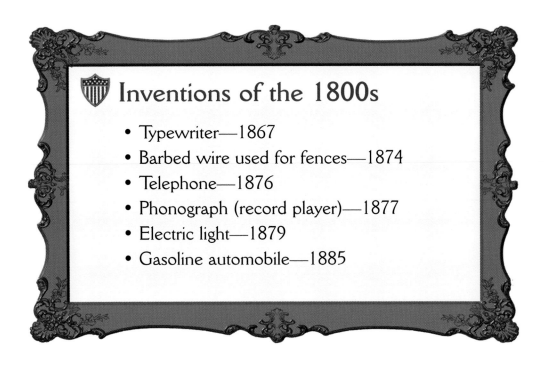

## Inventions of the 1800s

- Typewriter—1867
- Barbed wire used for fences—1874
- Telephone—1876
- Phonograph (record player)—1877
- Electric light—1879
- Gasoline automobile—1885

During the middle 1800s, only a small number of people lived in American cities. The majority of Americans spent their time farming, ranching, mining, settling lands, or making goods to sell. Many products were made by hand. Only one product could be made at a time this way. It took a long time to make many goods. As a result, many businesses remained small.

The American Civil War started in 1861 and ended in 1865. This was a war between the Northern and Southern states. This war changed the way Americans made things.

The locomotive steam engine first appeared in the 1830s. By the 1880s, these huge locomotives carried farmers' produce to market. "Iron horses" ran on tracks that connected every major city in the United States. Locomotives hauled their own fuel to keep the engine fire making steam.

Americans started using machines to make things. Machines made things much more quickly than a person could make them by hand. This allowed goods such as boots and guns to be sent to fighting troops. People controlled the machines. The machines were in buildings called factories. The development of this factory system is also known as the industrial boom.

After the war, businesses began using machines and factories to make other goods. A business could make more money if it had more goods to sell. This allowed businesses to grow. As a company grew, more employees were needed. Large factories hired hundreds of workers. More and more immigrants from other countries came to America to find work. Many early cities grew around factories and centers of industry.

The industrial boom of the 1800s caused many problems. Americans and new immigrants crowded into cities. They crowded into those areas where it was cheapest to live. These areas became slums. Life was dangerous and unclean in slums. People living in slums often became thieves. Many people could not even afford food.

Many workers lived in slums because they did not make very much money, even though they spent most of their time at work. They worked as many as sixteen hours each day. They did not get to enjoy extra activities such as strolling through the park. If a worker complained, a company would replace that worker with an immigrant or unemployed worker. To help their families buy food, many children worked in the factories instead of going to school.

Rural people moved to the city for jobs in factories. Their new work paid poorly. Most lived in bad conditions. This illustration shows people living in shacks in New York City's Central Park. The Populist Party tried to help factory workers live better.

Business and company owners did not live in slums. They lived very rich lives. Many had mansions and sent their children to private schools. The rich made fortunes that kept getting bigger.

Many businesses took advantage of poor and working-class people. Business owners could pay their workers whatever they wanted. They could also charge whatever they wanted for goods and services. Railroad companies became very powerful. They could charge whatever they wanted for fares. They charged farmers high prices to ship farming products and goods. Some railroad companies gave discounts to big business customers while charging high fares to regular people and farmers.

# 2
# Movement for the People

During the middle and late 1800s, factory workers began asking for better working conditions. They began to unite in unions. Unions are organizations that educate workers about their rights. Unions speak to business owners and managers. They ask for better working conditions on behalf of their members. Many early attempts to unionize did not work. This is because companies could easily replace union workers with nonunion workers or immigrants.

Middle-class and working-class Americans knew that the American system needed to be changed. New laws were needed to control big business. New laws could force businesses to treat workers fairly. These same laws could force the railroad companies to be fair to farmers and individual customers. Only the government could make these laws, however, so the people turned their attention to government officials and politicians.

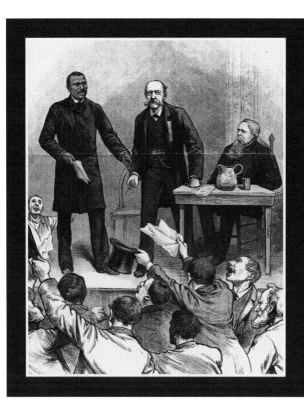

Knights of Labor leader Terence Powderly (*pictured in the center, standing*) fought for workers' rights. His labor organizations forced politicians to look at poor working conditions. The Knights of Labor also fought industry for better wages. Only with a proper income could workers expect to better their lives.

Government officials and politicians are supposed to represent the American people. Americans are not only the poor and working classes but also the wealthy. It was difficult for the government to balance the needs of all Americans. The government had to help businesses grow. It also had to help individual citizens, including both the rich and the poor.

Unfortunately, in the 1800s, many politicians and government officials were wealthy businessmen. Many government

Often, politicians would promise workers a better life while campaigning for election. After they were elected, though, these politicians would work to profit big business. Only after workers themselves united did government start working for them, as well.

jobs were given to friends instead of qualified people. As a result, it was hard to get laws passed to control business because many officials favored big business. Some officials were paid to vote against laws to control business. This was illegal, but officials did it anyway.

Reform means to correct or change something. Working-class Americans wanted to reform government and business. They wanted both to be honest and fair. When people unite for a common cause, such as reform, it is called a movement.

The movement for reform of government and business grew very strong in the 1880s and 1890s.

One way to cause reform was to elect honest officials and politicians into the government system. The government system was—and is—made of local, state, and national units. Dishonest officials were in all units. While some honest officials were able to help the American people, not enough of them were getting elected. Many people decided it would be easier to fight dishonest government practices by making new political parties.

A political party is an organized group of people who want to participate in government. Each party has its own goals and hopes for America. This is also known as a party platform. Each American decides which party he or she wants to support. He or she does so by learning about the party and its platform.

During the middle and late 1800s, two main political parties existed. These were the Democrats and the Republicans, which are still our main parties today. An example of a platform goal was the Republican stance against slavery. The party actually grew out of the anti-slavery movement. Americans who were strongly against slavery would most likely support the Republican Party and any Republican officials.

PLATFORMS ILLUSTRATED.

Before the 1880s, Democrats and Republicans only talked about farm reform. They did little to help farmers, though. This 1864 picture shows politicians from the Democratic National Convention. Neither workers nor farmers thought either political party looked out for their interests.

Members of political parties compete against each other in elections. The elections are for positions such as senator and mayor. The American people vote party members into these positions. When a party member is elected into a position, he or she fights for the party's goals, or platform.

Farmers and workers united in 1892 to form a new party. They did this because they felt that the Democratic and Republican Parties were not doing enough for them. They felt that a new platform with new goals was needed. This platform would protect the rights of the working class. The farmers and workers formed the Populist Party, also known as the People's Party. Those who supported the Populist Party were a part of the Populist movement.

# 3
## The Omaha Platform

The beliefs and goals of the Populist movement and Populist Party were listed in the Omaha Platform. The Omaha Platform was a written document that was adopted on July 4, 1892, in Omaha, Nebraska. When something is adopted, it means that it becomes official. By the time that the Omaha Platform was adopted, the Populist movement had already gained national support from many people.

The Populist movement is also known as populism. Farmers in the Midwest, South, and West started populism. During the 1870s and 1880s, these farmers had had many problems. The farmers were losing money on their crops. It was also getting more expensive to operate the farms. The railroad companies were charging high freight rates. Many of these farmers united together in the Farmers' Alliance.

This cartoon shows a farmer asking Uncle Sam (the U.S. government) for money to help keep his farm working. Farmers all through the Midwest demanded reform. They wanted fair transportation costs for their crops. They also wanted government loans to keep their farms running. These were the same kinds of help that big business already got from government.

The Farmers' Alliance was an organization formed in 1875. Its members asked government officials for help during the 1880s. They wanted the government to make more money. They wanted the government to give more money to American businesses, industries, and individuals. If Americans had more money to spend, they could then afford to pay the correct value for the crops. This would prevent farmers from losing money on crops. The Farmers' Alliance also wanted the government to take

control of the railroad industry. This would allow farmers to pay the correct fares for shipping freight and goods.

In July 1890, more than 800 officials met at Bohanan's Hall in Lincoln, Nebraska. The officials met to form a new party. Many of these officials belonged to the Farmers'

By 1890, farmers knew they had to unite to force the government to reform. They helped form the People's (Populist) Party. Party candidates won state elections in Nebraska. Shown here are members of the party convention held in Columbus, Nebraska. After winning control of the state legislature, the party looked toward the national elections.

Alliance. They called the party the Independent People's Party, which was later changed to the Populist Party. They used many of the goals of the Farmers' Alliance. They also wanted the government to control the telegraph and telephone industries, as well as for labor and factory workers to be given an eight-hour workday. At that time,

## Populists Take Over Nebraska

In the Nebraska state elections of November 1890, Populist Party candidates won many positions in government. The Republican Party had won elections since Nebraska had become a state in 1867, but the people of Nebraska now supported the Populist platform. The party gained control of Nebraska's state legislature.

The elected Populist officials then passed important laws. They passed laws that gave free textbooks to schools and made the education of children a priority. They also passed a law that allowed workers and laborers to go home after an eight-hour workday.

workers often worked more than twelve hours a day. The officials also elected party candidates for the upcoming state elections of 1890.

Other People's Party meetings took place in cities such as Cincinnati, Ohio, and Saint Louis, Missouri, during 1891. The party was soon growing and receiving national support. In July 1892, the first national convention, or meeting, took place in Omaha, Nebraska. The purpose of the convention was to make the Populist Party as strong and important as the Democratic and Republican Parties. The party members would officially decide the Populist platform. The members would also elect Populist candidates for the presidency and vice presidency of the United States.

The Populist platform was drafted (written) by Ignatius Donnelly (1831–1901), a former Republican congressman from Minnesota. The draft that Donnelly made was called the Omaha Platform. The Omaha Platform started with a preamble, or introduction. The introduction listed the failings of the government and the hopes of the party. Platform goals were listed under a section called "Platform." Extra goals and issues that the national convention agreed upon but did not need to include in the

In 1892, James B. Weaver ran for president of the United States. He was the first Populist Party candidate for president. Weaver got more than one million votes. He did not win, but his support forced Congress to notice farmers' demands.

platform were listed in another section. This section was called "Expressions of Sentiments."

The members at the national convention decided that James K. Weaver from Iowa should run for president of the Unites States. They elected James G. Field from Virginia to run for the vice presidency. The candidates did not win the election, but they did receive more than one million popular votes. This helped to show the government that the issues of the Populist movement were important.

This is an illustration of Democrat William Jennings Bryan giving his "Cross of Gold" speech. He ran for president in 1896 with the support of the Populist Party. Getting national party support helped the farmers even more in the 1890s.

In 1896, William Jennings Bryan from Nebraska was nominated for the 1896 presidential election. He was a Democrat who supported the Populist platform. The Populists joined with Democrats to support Bryan. Many Populists who believed that the party should not support a Democratic candidate left the party, and Bryan lost the election. While the Populist Party was active, no Populist was ever elected to the presidency.

# 4
# The Legacy

The Populist Party formed because its members believed that the nation was on the "verge of moral, political, and material ruin." The preamble of the Omaha Platform stated what was wrong with the country. It said that the government was dishonest. It said that the common worker had no voice or rights. It warned that the working conditions of America were getting worse and worse.

The Populist Party had many members who believed in America and the American government. They were passionate about America's future. They were worried that the government was allowing big business to keep the poor from having better lives. Donnelly wrote in the preamble that from the same place of government injustice came "two great classes—tramps and millionaires." What he meant was that these two classes were formed because of government injustice.

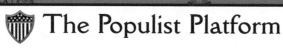

# The Populist Platform

- Farmers and workers should unite to make American life better.
- Farmers and workers have the same enemies: those who take advantage and steal from the working class.
- The government should own and control the railroad, telephone, and telegraph industries.
- The government should help with the financial problems of the working class.
- Money should be kept in the hands of the people, and people should not be heavily taxed by the government.
- Land should not be owned by non-Americans. Extra, unused land owned by railroads and other companies should be given to American settlers only.

Populists wanted the power of the government to be stronger. They wanted a fair government that was powerful enough to end poverty, dishonesty in business, and acts of oppression. Oppression is the treatment of a person in a cruel way. This power would mean that the government could control big business and stop oppressive acts against the common American.

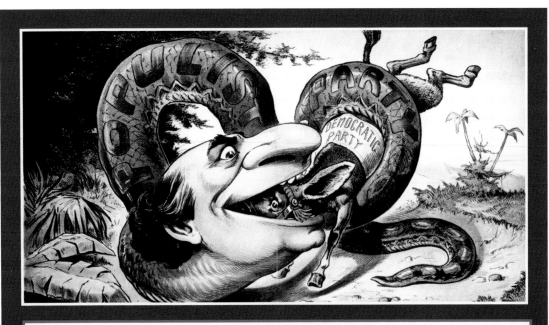

This 1900 political cartoon shows William Jennings Bryan as a snake swallowing the Democratic Party donkey. Bryan had gained such popular support that the Democrats could no longer ignore people's demands. Working-class problems became a Democratic issue. The Democratic Party has since become the party of the working class.

Populists not only wanted to reform government and big business, they also wanted other political parties to be reformed. They felt that the Republican and Democratic Parties were too worried about power. The common American was forgotten in the power struggle. Members of the Populist movement believed that both Republicans and Democrats were guilty of acting against the interests of the working class. Many Populists were able to convince Republicans and Democrats to support Populist issues. This was one of their greatest accomplishments.

The Populist movement was one of many movements in American history. The Populists were able to bring about some changes in America. Unfortunately, the party lasted less than fifteen years. Membership and power quickly declined after the 1896 presidential election. Members began to support either of the main parties that had adopted Populist goals. The Populist movement had ended by

The Populist Party and its movement had ended by 1904. Its support of working class issues helped clean up city streets. Factory workers began to earn higher wages. They could help improve their neighborhoods. Crime in cities went down. Life in the cities improved.

1904. It was replaced by the progressive movement and the New Deal era. This era brought about the greatest reform in government and business.

Although the party died out, many of its goals were adopted by new movements and the Republican and Democratic Parties as well. During the 1900s, Populist goals were accomplished, even though the Populist Party no longer existed. These goals were:

- Direct election of United States senators.
- Voter ability to propose laws and vote on laws (this is known as initiative and referendum).
- Graduated income tax: high incomes of the wealthy were taxed more heavily than low incomes of the poor.
- The eight-hour workday.

Today the word "populist" is used to describe politicians who do not fit into the traditional political party structure (Republican or Democrat). Some of these politicians ask for direct support from the people rather than from a party. Other politicians are called populist because they have political views and ideas that are new or uncommon. They may support issues from both the Republican and Democratic Parties. President Jimmy Carter, Vice President Hubert H. Humphrey, and Governor Jesse Ventura of Minnesota have been called populists.

# Glossary

convention (**kun-VEN-shun**)   A large gathering of people who have the same interests.

frontier (**frun-TEER**)   The edge of a settled country, where the wilderness begins.

industrial boom (**in-DUS-tree-ul BOOM**)   A time in history when factories and businesses grew quickly to make a country rich.

movement (**MOOV-ment**)   A group of people who have joined together to support a cause.

oppression (**uh-PREH-shun**)   The cruel, unjust treatment of people.

platform (**PLAT-form**)   The statement of beliefs of a group of people.

political party (**puh-LIH-tih-kul PAR-tee**)   An organized group of people who control or seek to control a government.

populism (**PAH-pyoo-lih-zum**)   The movement that supported reform of government and big business.

**Populist Party** (**PAH-pyoo-list PAR-tee**)   A political party that was formed to protect the rights of farmers and the working class.

**reform** (**ree-FORM**)   To improve, correct, or change something that is unsatisfactory.

**slum** (**SLUM**)   An area of a city that is crowded and dirty, where the poor live.

# Web Sites

Due to the changing nature of Internet links, the Rosen Publishing Group, Inc., has developed an online list of Web sites related to the subject of this book. This site is updated regularly. Please use this link to access the list:

http://www.rosenlinks.com/aistc/popa

# Primary Source Image List

**Page 6:** Photograph of Midland Terminal Depot, Victor, Colorado, circa 1895. Housed at the Denver Public Library, Denver, Colorado.

**Page 8:** 1869 *Harper's Weekly* illustration by D. E. Wyand of New York City's poor living in Central Park.

**Page 11:** Nineteenth-century woodcut illustration of Knights of Labor leader Terence Powderly.

**Page 12:** *Before the Election*, an 1849 illustration appearing in *Godey's Magazine*.

**Page 14:** 1864 lithograph of Democratic National Convention held in Chicago. Housed at the Library of Congress, Washington, D.C.

**Page 17:** Bernhard Gillam lithograph of farmer getting mortgage from Uncle Sam, in 1891 issue of *Judge*. Housed at the Library of Congress, Washington, D.C.

**Page 18:** 1890 photograph by Solomon D. Butcher of Independent People's (Populist) Party state convention in Columbus, Nebraska.

**Page 21:** Engraving of James B. Weaver, People's (Populist) Party candidate for president in 1892, circa 1880s.

**Page 22:** Illustration of William Jennings Bryan "Cross of Gold" speech, circa 1896.

**Page 25:** *Swallowed!* by J. S. Pughe, 1900 color lithograph. Housed at the Library of Congress, Washington, D.C.

**Page 26:** *Ghetto Scene: The Real Slums*, a photograph circa 1902 from the Seidman Photo Service.

# Index

# About the Author

Bernadette Brexel is a journalist and photographer from Omaha, Nebraska. She attended the University of Nebraska and Parsons in Paris.